# 7 HARD TRUTHS
## TRUTHS
### — OF —
# HEALING

## A GUIDE TO DOING IT ANYWAY

D1525542

## IMANI ADEGBUYI

Book Design by HMDpublishing

Hi, I'm Imani!

This book isn't about me, so I won't start our relationship by rattling off a list of titles, accolades, and unnecessary credentials – because none of those things are why I wrote this or why you're reading.

Think of me as the quiet coworker you kind of know, the pleasant neighbor who doesn't say much, the friend from college you spent a lot of time with but aren't quite sure where they live now or what they do – that's me. I've always lived under the radar, and honestly, I prefer it that way. The reality is I've been on a lifelong journey of healing, and solitude became my friend and greatest gift.

I grew up in NYC and the DMV; I'm definitely an east coast city girl with a dream of moving to Cali one day. I've been blessed to have some really awesome family who love and support me and friends who've become family over time. But I've also endured a lot of pain, loss, and suffering over the course of my life.

It wasn't until the infamous Covid-19 pandemic that I "woke up" and realized if I didn't do something drastically different, the rest of my life would look similar to everything I was trying to avoid. That's why I wrote this book – first to process my own journey, but second to help you on yours.

I just wish someone sat me down and had a real conversation with me about what to expect on this journey called healing *before* I started. This book is meant to empathize with you but also help you in the areas where I got stuck.

If you remember nothing else, remember we're in this together, I've been and am where you are, and I promise you there is a peace that comes from the progress you're making. Be kind to yourself on this journey to discover the hope you need to keep healing and becoming the beautiful soul you already are. But first, we've got to talk about the hard truths, hardships, and hassle of healing. Let's get to it.

# CONTENTS

# INTRODUCTION

Sometimes healing can be a painfully cyclical process. This book isn't a facetious attempt to inspire you that healing is simply a mindset you just need to tap into. This is a real and raw reflection guide to the hardest parts of healing and my two cents on how to keep going, or at least how I've done it.

I'm intentionally writing this from a hard place. I don't have the answers, but I do have a desire to help others feel seen, if this whole "healing journey" has been much harder than expected. You are not alone. By the time you're reading this, I've made some more progress, just like you will, but I'm nowhere near done. This is for the person who's only known how to endure, yet you struggle through your own process. After all you've been through, this shouldn't be as hard as it is, but here we are. It's okay; I get it.

For some reason, this quote has stuck with me lately – "If you're going through hell, keep going; why would you stop there?"

If all you can do is muster up the strength to wake up, get dressed, and go to work, do it. You're one step, one hour, one day closer to your breakthrough. I wish I could tell you how much longer, but I don't know either. I pray that you find just enough strength today to make it to tomorrow. No, survival is never the goal, but sometimes, that's your absolute best, and that's okay.

So, here's the thing, I'm the type of person that likes to overprepare and analyze as many contingencies as possible, all my Type A people can relate. The only surprises I like are cashapp notifications and birthday gifts. Anywho, I reallllyyyy wish someone told me the hard truths about healing! I don't think that would've changed my decision, but at least I wouldn't have been blindsided by all the backlash. Sound relatable? The one time you actually make yourself a priority, it's as if the world is against you.

Before I go any further, I have to be honest with you…true healing is utterly impossible without God. He is the only person that provides the depth of never-ending hope you desperately need just to make it to the next day. If you picked up this book in search of freedom and not some irrelevant religion, please hear me out. God doesn't want you to follow some arbitrary rules or strive for perfectionism; He just wants to know you, love you, and have a personal relationship with you. As hard as life has been for some of us, I promise you it is harder on your own. If you're not convinced, that's okay, this book isn't intended to convert you or shame you, but I couldn't share my truth without being transparent about my anchor. The only reason I can still press on to the next day is because deep down in me, I trust what I can't see and put my faith in someone greater than any modern-day self-care life hack, and His name is Jesus.

So back to why you're here – the ugly truth no one ever told us about healing. Here are my 7 hard truths. Take some time to read through them first, then go back to answer each question and reflect. I wanted this to be a useful and practical resource for you, so read, reflect, and repeat it as often as you need to. Copy the prompts to your journal, dry ease board, or whatever works for you. There's only one rule – you must, must, must be 100% honest with yourself. We're on this journey together, and I want us to leave better than the way we came. Breathe, and let's get started.

# HARD TRUTH #1

# GUILT

**H**ere's a humbling definition for you about guilt – feelings of deserving blame, especially for imagined offenses or from a sense of inadequacy. Does anyone else feel affirmed but checked? Just me, okay...

*Imagined offenses*, wow. Apparently, some of the things we're in inner turmoil about aren't even real? Remember that phrase you probably heard in adolescence – "perception is reality." I guess that applies to us too. Just something to think about.

Nevertheless, feeling guilty has been the hardest and heaviest load I've carried in this healing journey. It took so much strength to finally speak up and decide I would choose myself, only to find out my emotions would constantly and relentlessly sabotage me. I'm hoping you can't relate because you're reading this as a pre-warning to the journey you're embarking on. But if you can relate and you're totally confused about how *you* aren't even on your side, I get it.

Guilt is a trap; it never ends, it's never satisfied, and when you give in just a little, it becomes a powerful vacuum dragging you to a place you don't want to be in. Guilt sometimes feels like a sucker punch at the end of a long day. It's the last thing you need and always knows right when to show up. Guilt is versatile in a very annoying way; it runs ramped independently in your mind and engulfs your closest friends and family. It knows precisely which childhood memory to trigger, and presses the right wound every time.

If you're not even sure what you're feeling is guilt, sometimes it's an overwhelming sense of regret for doing what you know was right but feel bad about. So, what do we do with guilt?

Here's my two cent – Address guilt head on, never avoid it, and always indignantly refuse to embrace it! You've got to practice getting irrational fears out of your head. They thrive on putting in double time on the treadmill of your conscience. For me, dealing with guilt meant journaling and venting as long as I need to. And yes, occasionally, that does mean an extra cupcake or two. Identifying healthy coping mechanisms is important too, but one thing at a time.

This is the part where you participate now ●. Here are some prompts to help you recognize, process, and deal with the guilt you're feeling.

# REFLECTION QUESTIONS:
## HARD TRUTH #1 – GUILT

1. What just happened that made me feel guilty? Describe the situation from beginning to end.

2. Who was involved? Has this person done or said something that made me feel guilty before?

3. Is this situation a pattern or an isolated incident? What else has happened recently?

4. Which part do I feel the worst about? Why does that make me feel so terrible?

5. What harm do I feel I caused?

6. Did I actually cause harm, or is this a perceived offense? If I did cause harm, what are the objective facts to support that claim?

7. If my friend described the situation above, would I think they should feel guilty?

If you've gotten to the end of these questions and you don't feel any lighter, go back to #1 and #7 and journal again. Guilt is a strong force, but it always loses its grip with time. Take your time with this one.

# HARD TRUTH #2
# THE RAGING INNER CHILD

**I**f you've been in therapy for any amount of time, which I highly recommend, you probably guessed this next one. No, I am not a therapist, but my life has definitely benefited from a really great one – you know who you are; THANK YOU!

Here's a definition I like – "Our inner child is a part of ourselves that's been present from the beginning; it can often recall good experiences as well as childhood fears, traumas, neglect, or significant loss. (https://integrativepsych.co/new-blog/what-is-an-inner-child)

Here's my definition - the 5-year-old version of you was just old enough to remember but not quite old enough to comprehend. You remember some significant life events that still feel real today, but much of your day-to-day feels blurry. In the context of healing – here's the problem, that inner child rages against anything and anyone that feels unsafe, including you.

The 5-year-old version of you will throw a complete mental tantrum at the thought of embracing something new and untested – especially something as audacious as healing a deep wound. That little kid inside is like a toddler with no nap, no snacks, and no toy – highly agitated and destructive. It seeks to destroy every possible threat to its normal. Just like a child can't discern the difference between wants and needs, the younger you cannot rationalize how the discomfort of healing is better that the "peace" of pain.

So, after you find yourself crawling out of the pit of guilt, here comes this small but mighty Tasmanian devil ripping through what's left of you, desperately begging you to hit the reset button and forget you ever promised yourself to embark on this healing journey. It's the ultimate type of sabotage, manipulating every sentimental and painful memory to coerce you into quitting. Just when you thought you've suppressed or processed that memory enough, you're very quickly reminded how much your brain and heart hate change and are always willing to revert, just like a curly girl's silk press on a humid summer day.

Here's your tip – Soothe it but don't save it. Comfort your inner child with reassurance that the pain of change is only temporary and the truth of the situation. You're entitled to your feelings, but that doesn't make them factual. Remind yourself of the pure facts. Then, don't rescue your inner child. That reversion you so desperately desire is a hoax; it will give you temporary relief, and then you'll find yourself 2 steps forward and 10 steps back. The promise of comfort is an illusion, don't fall for it.

# REFLECTION QUESTIONS:
## Hard Truth #2 – The Raging Inner Child

1. What part of your healing journey do you feel the urge to stop engaging in?

2. Why does doing that thing make you feel so uncomfortable?

3. In your mind, what would be more comfortable right now?

4. Is that real comfort or avoidance? Ask yourself, what end result are you trying to achieve?

5. What will be the immediate outcome if you stop and go back to the place that feels safer right now? What will you feel then?

6. Now, what will be the long-term outcome of remaining in that "safer" place? Is that a place you want to stay?

7. What truth can you tell yourself at this moment to help you overcome the desire to quit?

8. Why did you start this healing journey in the first place?

9. Encourage yourself with recounting some progress you recently made.

10. Identify the lies the younger you wants you to believe about turning back.

# ESTABLISHING NEW BOUNDARIES

I know, boundaries, boundaries, boundaries. They're apparently the one thing your life has been missing all this time. Everyone has their opinion about all the boundaries you should have in your life and how simple it is to wake up one day just do it. "You set the boundaries in your life; you're the only one in control; other people can't define their place in your life." Blah, blah, blah, you get the point, all well-meaning advice that unintentionally dismisses the complexity of whatever relationship you're already struggling to navigate.

Here's what no one told me that I desperately wish I knew – choosing yourself will cause significant agitation to everyone and everything that was used to you choosing them first. One of my favorite quotes says it this way – "The only people who get upset about you setting boundaries are the ones who were benefiting from you having none" – Unknown

A harsh reality, but true. Nevertheless, dealing with the backlash of making yourself a priority is hard. This one is probably the hardest part of the process for me. Waking up one day, exhausted from a lifestyle absent of self-care and healing, is the exact motivation you need to get started. But the constant defending of your physical, mental, and emotional health is exhausting! Those you love the most are sometimes the same ones that make your choice to choose you to seem wrong. And there are more days than you're comfortable admitting; you'd prefer to endure the familiar pain of suffering rather than fight this new battle of perseverance. The fight against yourself to believe you deserve better was hard enough. Sis/Bro, I feel you; I really do. I'm intentionally writing this from my own place of exhaustion because it's time for more real conversations about the impact of healing.

Disrupting the patterns of normalcy are not easy. It's far from impossible, but it does require you to fight. Sometimes you have to fight yourself and the voices in your head that are begging you to revert back to the passive, self-neglecting person you were; and other times you have to fight other's over-critical assessments of your needs. Some may never understand, and you should be prepared to make every necessary adjustment in those relationships, which might mean temporary or permanent separation. Prepare yourself for the battle, and do not fight alone.

Here's the tip – Accept but adjust. Give the people in your life grace and time to process what's happening. You've probably spent months or even years reflecting on everything you've needed that you never got in your relationships with others. But to your loved ones, this is all new information, or its relevance is a new level of insight. Remember, they don't really know this version of you yet. They're still trying to understand how their perception of the last 10, 20, 30, and 40+ years of relationship with you was totally different from your experience. If they truly love you, their pushback is not malicious, it's fear and a defense mechanism to keep the relationship status quo or safe, so they'll need some time.

Accept where they are, accept how they're reacting, accept that change takes time, but always remain firm in what you need. Your biggest enemy is your own adverse nature to conflict. Having a boundary one day and then going back on your word the next is the deepest form of self-sabotage. You undermine your own credibility and making progression even more difficult on yourself. In those tempting moments to give up, reflect on what life has really been like for you without these boundaries. If you are not intentional and dogmatically consistent about putting yourself first, you cannot expect a different result.

# REFLECTION QUESTIONS:
## HARD TRUTH #3 – ESTABLISHING NEW BOUNDARIES

1. What boundaries have you been successful in implementing?
2. Which boundary are you struggling to implement the most?
3. What about that boundary is more challenging than others?
4. If implemented successfully, what is the expected outcome of this new boundary?
5. What do you think will happen if you do not implement this boundary?
6. What has your experience been so far without this boundary in place?
7. In what ways have you suffered physically, mentally, emotionally, and/or spiritually without this boundary in place?
8. What feelings are coming to the surface when you think about your need for this boundary vs. the needs of others around you?
9. Are you falling back into the traps of guilt and people-pleasing?
10. Create a strategy for your boundary:
    a. What is the boundary I need to implement?
    b. Why is this important to me?
    c. What do I want to remind myself of when I'm struggling?
    d. Who will be my accountability partner for this?
    e. What do I anticipate being the biggest challenge?
    f. What will be my response to that challenge?
    g. How will I know the boundary was successful?
    h. How will I celebrate myself for sticking to it?

# THE FIGHT FOR CENTER STAGE

This one here, man. You never really know what someone thinks about their position, relevance, or influence in your life until you try to make adjustments that aren't in line with their idea of how things should be. It's *almost* a little comical when you realize how much control people think they should or do have over your life. The level of entitlement some people develop because of their position or proximity to you can be extremely frustrating, yet again becoming another harsh reality you must address.

The people in your circle are used to a certain level of predictability with you. When you decide you need a change and you follow through with it, you disrupt their world. And suddenly, what was simply you putting yourself first, becomes a battle for who's emotions and comfort are more important. It's the trifecta of guilt, shame, and people-pleasing all in one. It's the fight for the center stage – who will be the focal point. And most likely, all this time, it has never been you.

In some cases, the person does truly love you, but you'll have to carefully assess did they love you or did they love the benefits of your presence in their life. I could speak to that, but that would be a totally separate book. In unique situations, there really is genuine love present, like with a parent or close friend, but they are only used to loving you on their terms, in ways they've dictated, with little or no input from you. And your healing desperately requires disrupting that cycle of letting others define how they will treat you; but that disruption does not come cheap. It is very expensive – the emotional and mental investment it takes to remind yourself that focusing on your needs is no longer negotiable in the face of opposition is not to be taken lightly. The people you love the most will do and say almost anything to plead their cases for the #1 spot on your priority list, and you must be steadfast in your "no".

At its worst, that disruption to the status quo can mean you're the bud of jokes, your insecurities become the target of angry outbursts and heart-wrenching name-calling, the complete dismissal of your needs and distortion of your reputation among others. It is rough, and depending on how attached that other person is to their version of reality, it can be the most harmful experience in your relationship with them. Somehow, the years of neglecting your needs are nothing compared to the pain you have or will endure because you dared to choose yourself. After all, when you turn on the lights in a mansion that's never had electricity, who knows what you'll uncover.

My tip is simple this time – Ignore the noise. The insults, redirects, deflecting, low-blows, and full tantrums, ignore it all. Always consider the source and reasons why they're saying or doing something. 99.99999999% of the time, it's really not about you; it's their attachment and familiarity to the unhealed version of you – and most of all the fear associated with change.

# REFLECTION QUESTIONS:
## HARD TRUTH #4 – THE FIGHT FOR CENTER STAGE

1. Who or what has been on the center stage of your life?
   a. Don't allow guilt or shame to cause dishonesty with yourself. You need to expose the truth to truly move forward.

2. What are the circumstances that led to them being there?

3. How has being second in your own life impacted you?

4. What (do you think) will happen when you make adjustments to prioritize yourself?

5. If you've endured any unpleasant reactions to standing up for yourself, evaluate the source – who are they? How do they see their role in your life? In what ways do you feel controlled by them? What would you like their actual role to be?

6. How have others in center stage benefited from you neglecting yourself?

7. How have you suffered from you neglecting yourself?

8. This change will be the hardest part of your journey – who will encourage you along your journey and help hold you accountable?

9. How will you build a new community of like-minded support?
   a. I highly recommend searching Facebook groups ●

# HARD TRUTH #5

# THE DOUBLE LIFE

**W**hile you are healing and going through the hardest transitional season of your life, the reality is 95% of the people you interact with have absolutely no idea. Another 3% are close enough to pick up on your bad days, and the last 1% is your inner circle, who know almost everything and are amazed at all you're juggling. It feels like you're living two totally different lives – the one where you're pretending you're fine and one where you're totally raw and borderline falling apart. The reality is that parts of your journey require this weird double agent living. Your vulnerability in this season, and really always, should be managed with prudence.

It's already exhausting to face all the unanticipated impacts of choosing to love yourself, but to have to do that every day and plaster a smile on your face at work, church, or sorority events, the extra energy required is pulling from an already depleted place. If you can relate to pretending your home life was fine as a child when it really wasn't, then this might not be as difficult for you. But, even if you're used to "faking it till you make it", the mental gymnastics it takes to make wise and sound decisions despite the insurmountable inner turmoil in your heart is additionally exhausting.

A part of healing is evaluating those in your life and making the necessary adjustments and appropriate relational assignments to each person. Sometimes that means adjusting your proximity and expectations of those who are unable or unwilling to meet the requirements of what you need. "Everyone is equally valuable, but everyone does not add equal value to your life". I highly recommend Relational Intelligence by Dharius Daniels to help you assess and adjust all of your relationships.

So, you're right in protecting your vulnerability by not oversharing with those who have not earned the privilege of intimacy with you, but it's hard because you're not *you* right now. And you're certain you won't go back to the unhealed version of yourself, but if you're being honest, you also don't know who is on the other side of this transformational healing.

Here's my tip – Define and confide in your circle. Whether you need to vent, seek advice, or get encouragement, find a few people you can trust and check in regularly. Share your wins and your struggles with those who will walk alongside you and not sabotage your evolution.

You also need rest and recreation. Take naps and get a healthy amount of sleep each night. If you can afford a week on an island resort, go for it! If you can't, just turn your phone off for the weekend and decompress. Your heart, mind, and soul need time to exhale.

# REFLECTION QUESTIONS:
## HARD TRUTH #5 – THE DOUBLE LIFE

1. Describe the person you used to be.
2. Ask yourself who do you want to become?
3. Where do you need to steward your vulnerability?
4. Where and with whom can you be "naked"?
5. Who in your life has proven mature enough to handle your brokenness with care?
6. Who can you vent to today to avoid oversharing or feeling overwhelmed tomorrow?
   a. *If you can't think of anyone, journal in silence for at least 30 minutes*
7. In the next 30 days, what are your plans to recharge?
8. Have you taken time to discover yourself lately? What do you like? What really makes you happy? What things in your life do you want to start and stop? What do you want to revisit?
9. How can you incorporate small mental breaks throughout each day?
10. When envisioning the most authentic and healed version of yourself in the future – what advice would he/she give you right now?

# HARD TRUTH #6

# SHEDDING

I t feels lonely when you realize nothing you knew works and no human, except maybe your therapist, really understands the depth and complexity of your current struggle. This stage of intentional healing in your life is rewarding because you finally have insight into the "what and why" of your past. But there's also the downside of realizing you have to change your environment if you want lasting results in your life. Some call it – "the backside of the blessing."

Here you are, finally able to shed the weight of all the childhood trauma and failed relationships, only to realize that this next phase of your life requires you to embrace everything unfamiliar. You must create and maintain mental and physical distance from all the damaging people, places, and things you justified. Your emotions are still not on board, but your brain has enough new knowledge to know these adjustments are necessary.

But let's face it – our hearts and emotions are incredibly powerful. No matter how much we know the transition is necessary, it still sucks. For me, living in a new city in the middle of a global pandemic made something as simple as needing a hug or happy hour so far out of reach. You don't quite have the energy to form new meaningful friendships and sometimes you really don't want to be alone, but that's where you find yourself. Friday after Friday, you, your couch, and Netflix. Everything can't be explained in a text to your long-distance best friend; and facetime nor body pillows quite replace the warmth of another soul comforting you.

You're shedding everything you knew – internally and externally. You're trying to trust the process and not cheat the steps, but it is hard. The same silence of solitude opens both the depths of your sadness and endless unexplainable joy. Yes, you miss companionship, but not at the expense of your peace, wholeness, or sanity. You believe who you're becoming and what's ahead is better than what you left behind, and you're right.

Here's my tip – Date yourself. It might sound trivial, but hear me out. In this season, you need a little more solitude than usual to help you process everything happening. Yes, it's lonely, but it doesn't have to be miserable. Take yourself out somewhere once a week. Make time to enjoy the simple things in life that bring you joy. There is no magic pill that will make you forget all your worries and instantly feel amazing, but it is a great way to take your mind off the life you left behind and create great habits for the life ahead of you. This next version of you needs you to value self-care. The best part is, you'll discover new things about yourself too.

# REFLECTION QUESTIONS:
## HARD TRUTH #6 – SHEDDING

1. What do you miss about the past? Why?

2. What don't you miss?

3. What had to die in order to birth the new you?

4. List all the negative thoughts that come up when you think about how life used to be for you.

5. List all the positive things you're currently experiencing or looking forward to.

6. How can you create new meaningful experiences in your life this week?

7. Plan your next 3 dates – pick a date, location, and outfit. If you can squeeze in some pampering too – a fresh haircut or manicure will boost your mood ●

8. Remind yourself why you choose to keep healing today. What is the end result you're working toward? What picture of your future will encourage you in times of loneliness?

9. Who or what do you want to fill the new space in your life with?

10. Write a letter to the future you and tell him or her what this part of the journey is like. These letters will serve as a reminder that you have the ability to overcome your hardest moments.

# HARD TRUTH #7

# FADING FOCUS

ast but certainly not least, amid the most transformative meta-
morphosis of your life, the world around you still goes on, and
some days it's overwhelming trying to pay attention to both. In
addition to therapy, bound-setting, extensive journaling, and self-
care dates, you still have an exhaustive list of responsibilities in your
personal and professional life. You still want to celebrate life events
and major accomplishments of those you love. You still have your
list of annual goals and resolutions. And because you simply didn't
know how intense this healing process would be, you might even
begin to feel like you haven't made much progress. Especially if
you're a parent, spouse, or a leader in any capacity, your day-to-day
didn't ease up just because you decided to work on yourself. While
you made some adjustments, the reality is there's still a lot left you
need to focus on, in addition to your process, and that seems borderline impossible. It might even be the reason why you've avoid-
ed the pursuit of healing altogether or stopped abruptly. Friend,
no judgement here, ever. I just want you to know that the time is
always right to work on your life just as much as you work in everyone else's. Tomorrow is not promised to any of us, but you are
damaging yourself and those around you by refusing to lay down
burdens you were never meant to carry.

Between your emotions hijacking your heart, your friends and
family trying to figure out who you are now, the progressive un-
folding of your new identity; how in the world are you supposed to
focus on major projects at work, birthday parties, weight loss goals,
family vacations, and your best friend's wedding? It's not that you

don't care, but realistically, you don't have the same capacity you normally would. Your mental energy is invested in becoming the man or woman your destiny demands. Writing this book has been my own struggle of focus. As much as I wanted to write this to help you, it took much longer than I anticipated. Life happens, and that's okay. Simply pick up where you left off and keep going.

This tip is pretty simple, and if you remember nothing else you've read, remember — you owe yourself an inexhaustible amount of grace and patience right now. While you are certainly amazing, and possibly a superhero in disguise, you are still only one person. Some deadlines will be missed, some days you just won't feel like it, and some goals will have to be postponed. All of that is okay. You are not a failure; you are human. Each day you wake up, you have a new opportunity to refocus, reprioritize, and recenter. *You* are your priority right now, and if no one else affirms that for you, simply re-read this as often as you need to. You are not selfish for making time for yourself. You are deserving of the time you need to become who you always were underneath the rubble of life.

# REFLECTION QUESTIONS:
## HARD TRUTH #7 – FADING FOCUS

1. What are your top 5 priorities right now?

2. What is the outcome of not focusing on those 5 things right now?

3. What sacrifices do you need to make to maintain your focus?

4. What are the other things you're spending your time on that are not your top priorities?

5. Which priority are you struggling to focus on the most?

6. Where can you request help with something else you're responsible for?

7. What goals can be deferred until you have more capacity?

8. What is your motivation right now to keep pressing forward?

9. How can you reward yourself and celebrate small wins?

10. How will you practice grace and compassion with yourself?

# CONCLUSION

Healing is not a destination; we will never arrive. It's a journey with highs and lows, twists and turns, and who you are becoming is a masterpiece. In fact, you're simple uncovering the masterpiece you always were like the grand reveal of a beautiful sculpture. Some parts of the journey are dark, but there is beauty in ashes – the burning away of the pain and fear you once confused as your identity.

Feel free to revisit each truth as often as you need to. Each pain point you encounter on your healing journey is a new lesson and new knowledge you need to become the best version of yourself. Embrace it, accept it, and be relentless in your pursuit of the whole, happy, healthy you that's on the other side. You got this, I'm rooting for you.

# ACKNOWLEDGEMENTS

First and foremost, I give all thanks and adoration to the triune God, without whom I would never have the courage to share my story.

I'd like to thank my mom, whose unconditional and endless love has been one of the greatest blessings of my life. Mommy, thank you. For all you did and all you continue to do to make sure I become everything God intended for me to be. Thank you for your intentional efforts to cultivate me into the woman I am today.

A very special thank you to personal dream team – my pastor, my therapist, and my coach. You three have forever changed the trajectory of my life in ways I can't explain. My evolution and growth are directly connected to the investments you've made in your respective gifts. Your faithfulness to your assignments has indeed produced fruit in mine.

Last but certainly not least, I'd like to thank my friends and family. To those who have stuck by me in rough seasons, wiped my invisible tears, made space for my vulnerability, handled my mistakes with mercy, and kept pushing me never to give up. Thank you for seeing in me, what I couldn't see in myself. Thank you for meeting needs I didn't know I had. And even to those who chose to walk away, I truly wish you all the best and thank you for teaching me my own strength.

A special shoutout to the family of Alpha Nu Omega, Incorporated. May we never stop building up the kingdom and holding up the light, wherever God has called us.

Made in the USA
Middletown, DE
20 September 2022

10884612R00018